WOOD TURNING FOR THE GARDEN

WITH MIKE CRIPPS

PROJECTS FOR OUTDOORS

Text written with and photography
by Jeffrey B. Snyder

Schiffer Publishing Ltd

77 Lower Valley Road, Atglen, PA 19310

Dedication

To hobby wood turners everywhere.

Book Design by Audrey L. Whiteside

Printed in China
ISBN: 0-7643-0032-6

Published by Schiffer Publishing, Ltd.
77 Lower Valley Road
Atglen, PA 19310
Phone: (610) 593-1777
Fax: (610) 593-2002

Please write for a free catalog.
This book may be purchased from the publisher.
Please include $2.95 for shipping.
Try your bookstore first.

We are interested in hearing from
authors with book ideas on related subjects.

Contents

Acknowledgments

     I would like to thank the following for their contributions to these projects: For rustic timber in log form, Chadds Ford Tree Service, Chadds Ford, PA. Hardwood supplier, Wagon House Hardwood Lumber, Mendenhall, PA.

     I may be reached at the following address for wood turning supplies, courses in wood turning, or to chat about my books: Middlesex Woodcraft, 41 The Greenway, Ickenham, Middlesex, England, UB10 8LS, Phone: 01895 675070. (Courses for beginners in wood turning and wood turners' supplies by mail order. Callers welcome. Please phone before dropping in.)

Foreword

I have known Mike Cripps for many years and it is a particular pleasure to introduce him to you as the author of this book. He is a big hearted, jovial and highly talented turner who is particularly suited to lead you through the techniques he describes.

Mike and I first met at one of his early wood turning meetings held at a local Cricket Club. His enthusiasm for turning and willingness to help others encouraged a lot of members to improve technique and try other projects.

About a year later, after a lot of hard work, Mike became one of the founding members of the A.W.G.B. (The Association of Woodturners of Great Britain) which was launched in 1987 at the first Loughborough seminar.

In 1990, after being made redundant, Mike decided to set up his own turning school/wood and tool store. This has been a great success and hundreds of aspiring turners have passed through his classes, some now winning competitions, a tribute to Mike's teaching skills and encouragement.

The project in this book is good practice for any turner - just follow Mike's superb instructions and enjoy your turning.

Mac Kemp
Chairman
Middlesex Woodturners Association

About this Book — Wood Turning for the Garden with Mike Cripps Projects for Outdoors

It is common for wood turners to make items for home use. I am sure that you would easily be able to list at least fifty items for use inside the house. How many ideas could you compile for use in your *yard*?

I thought it would be fun to tackle some projects for this domain, so sadly neglected by us wood turners. Naturally, we will have to use a suitable type of wood and a treatment for protection against the elements.

The projects in this book are suitable for wood turners of most levels of ability. Hobbyists and professionals alike will enjoy the great experience of turning unseasoned timber, which is free from dust and needs virtually no sanding or difficult-to-apply glossy finish.

Garden Dibber

The first article in this book takes you through the steps for turning a garden dibber (an implement for making holes in the earth to insert bulbs or plants). An ornate garden dibber would make a useful and unusual present for that garden loving friend or relation. When word gets around, who knows, perhaps we will create a new trend among horticultural fans here in the United States and the simple garden dibber will be elevated to new-found importance in even the most famous potting sheds.

Making dibbers is great fun for practicing your spindle turning skills. They can be made from either seasoned or unseasoned timber, and they can be as pretty or as plain as you like.

Planters and Containers

Bowls and troughs can be made from unseasoned timber in the round. They are ideal to stand on garden walls and patios and have a natural beauty of their own when planted up with flowers.

Unseasoned wood is a low cost material alternative, it cuts easily and is great fun to turn. When finished, planters should be oiled and filled with earth straight away to prevent initial cracking by slowing the drying rate.

Another possibility, although not shown in step-by-step turning here, is to use the wood lathe to produce wall planters. The good thing about making these wall mounted objects is that for every one you turn in the round, two can be made just by sawing them in half. They have traditional and rustic appearance. When filled with trailing plants, they will brighten up a dull fence, wall or corner of your yard. Alternatively, they are good for housing useful objects such as hose parts, wire ties, or small tools.

Bird Nesting Boxes

Instead of a few pieces of rough timber nailed together, a nesting box turned from a round of unseasoned timber is elegant to look at and fun to make. It also provides a home for several generations of small birds. The size of the entry hole is important — one-and-one eighth inches is the size we use in England if we want to attract tits and keep out larger species such as sparrows. A little research will tell you the direction and habitat in which the box should be placed.

Barbecue Lamps

Although not one of the projects produced in this text, these small lamps are handy when dining outdoors with good company, good food and good wine. The soft light glow of a candle or an oil lamp makes this a lovely experience. Lamps can be made tall or short, chunky or delicate.

Whatever the size or shape, these lamps will enhance your table for the benefit of your guests — and yourself. After all, everybody looks better and more romantic in soft lighting, and there is also a good chance that nobody will notice how black the steak is!

I have a colleague in England who exports thousands of oil lamps to America every year, so I am sure your efforts will be well received.

Common Sense Information for Beginners to Wood Turning

Obtaining Knowledge

Before turning wood on your own, make the effort to watch someone else doing it and do not be afraid to ask questions. Most people that I have met who work in wood are friendly and are usually only too pleased to help someone starting in this rewarding hobby. Books and videos are, of course, a great way of obtaining knowledge of the subject; however, the best ways to learn are by either taking a 'Beginner's Course' or by getting some hands on experience if you can.

Buying Your First Wood Lathe

I am often asked, "Which lathe should I buy?" My answer is always, "Get the best that you can afford." Cheap imported lathes very often are noisy, this being caused by inferior electric motors that vibrate excessively. This vibration reverberates through the drive belt to the lathe headstock, which is usually clad in a thin, rattly casing. This vibration can be reduced by both easing the tension on the belt slightly and making sure all bolts and screws, including the bench securing bolts, are tight. It is well worth the effort to check these items over before using the machine.

Whether you buy new or second-hand, when looking for a reliable machine the following points are worth your consideration:

(a) Does the lathe have a heavy steel plate or cast head?

(b) Are the head and tailstock spindles hollow to allow the use of standard fittings (1 or 2 morse tapers)? This will save money as you will be able to buy 'off the shelf' lathe accessories.

(c) Place a drive centre in the headstock and a centre in the tailstock and check for alignment with the points. If they do not meet properly you will always drill oversized holes and have excess vibration.

(d) Place a mandrel or large accessory such as a drill chuck in the headstock and check for sideways movement. If the lathe has standard bearings, movement denotes a worn bearing. If, however, bearings are tapered roller types, this movement could be cured by adjustment.

(e) Check for side play in the tailstock where it located on the bed. If the tailstock is badly worn, the resultant side play will cause vibration and will result in inaccurate drilling.

(f) Make sure that the tool rest locks both on the bed and in its support securely and without the application of excess force on the securing levers. REMEMBER that you frequently move the tool rest.

(g) If buying second-hand, take a mental calculation of the chucks and accessories that come with it; usually it is the presence of these that makes a used lathe an attractive proposition as a new wood turning chuck can cost around $150 to $200. A drill chuck and live centres cost around $50, drives and mandrels $20 to $30 each when purchased new.

(h) Smell the motor to check for any burnt smells which indicate that the motor is already burnt out or is well on the way. Also, disconnect the belt and see if the motor runs quietly. A noisy motor usually means the bearings on the shaft need replacing.

Basic Turning Tools

The ROUGHING GOUGE, as the name implies, is used for roughing down from square to round. It is also used for the preliminary shaping work on spindle turning e.g. shallow curves and tapers. I find that it is also an excellent tool for flat areas when face plate turning.

A 3/4" roughing gouge is the ideal tool to start with. The approach to the wood should be as follows. Place the roughing gouge firmly on the tool rest with the blade pointing upwards. Lower the tip of the tool down slowly until the bevel rubs on the wood without the cutting edge coming into contact with the wood (this is what I call the no-cut position). Continue to lower the cutting edge down onto the wood until you obtain the first sign of a shaving. Only when this is obtained should you travel along the tool rest from left to right and vice versa to true up the wood between centres.

The PARTING TOOL is an essential tool. I would suggest that a 1/8" wide parting tool is the best to start with and will be the cheapest for spindle turning. The parting tool is used to make incisions into the wood at each end of a piece to provide a waste end which is discarded when the piece is parted off the lathe.

There are two basic methods employed when using the parting tool. The first involves pointing the tool upwards while sitting it firmly on the tool rest and pushing it in an upward direction. The second method is to start with the tool again sitting on the rest and slowly levering the tip downwards using the tool rest as a fulcrum. NEVER go below the level position and point the tool downwards as it could be pulled in towards the wood and jammed against the tool rest. However, whenever you are making deep parting cuts or grooves, always ensure that you make the cuts slightly wider than the tool so that it does not get gripped.

The parting tool is also useful for rolling beads and cutting recesses for chucks on faceplate work. If the parting tool is used on its side, flat on the tool rest, the point can be used to score decorative grooves in the wood using this scraping cut.

SPINDLE GOUGES come in a range of sizes from 1/8" to 3/4". Most commonly today they are made from round section bar but traditional or continental gouges are still being produced. These are made from pre-formed curved section steel.

The main uses for the spindle gouges are for forming beads and coves, rounding over and squaring up end grain. I would suggest a 3/8" is a good one to start with.

When cutting coves or hollows, point the centre of the gouge at the starting point, cutting down one side to just past the centre of the bottom of the cove and then repeat the process on the other side. By cutting down the hill, or from the largest toward the smallest diameter, you will be compressing together the fibres in the wood with the bevel while the cutting edge does its job. This will give you a good finish. Cutting uphill separates the fibres and leaves an inferior finish. REMEMBER, if you slowly swing the end of the handle in a circular motion, the shape of the cove will also have a round profile. To cut beads or balls the tool has to be rolled over, working again from the top toward the bottom with the bevel rubbing.

The SKEW CHISEL is probably the tool that takes a fair bit of practice before it is mastered. I would suggest that you purchase a 1" OVAL SKEW as this is a size that is good for planing and making beads and squaring ends. An oval skew is nicer to handle than a rectangular section skew as the corners tend to stick on any nicks or grooves in the tool rest.

To plane a cylinder to a smooth finish, raise the tool rest to centre height and position it as close as possible to the pre-roughed out cylinder. Place your thumb firmly on the tool rest just past the end of the wood and tuck the skew between the thumb and the tool rest. Now, using the short corner of the skew and not using any more than 1/8" from the point, the tool should be about 45 degrees to the wood. Obtain a shaving and travel along the tool rest. You may have to alter the angle of the tool or raise or lower the blade slightly. REMEMBER the shaving is the reward and the sign that you are cutting correctly. You will be able to cut coming back along the tool rest by holding the tool at the same angle.

To form beads with the skew chisel I prefer to use the long point and, as when cutting, only use the actual point and up to 1/8" from it. NEVER cut uphill. Start at the top of the bead, rolling the skew over as it cuts through 90 degrees with the blade vertical on completion of the cut at the base of the bead. When making beads or spheres, work on the right, then the left, repeating the process and bringing on both sides together. REMEMBER when cutting over beads etc., rub the bevel all the way — lifting the handle up as the cutting action goes down.

The BOWL GOUGE, as the name implies, is the tool for turning bowls. A 3/8" high speed steel gouge made from 1/2" round steel with a long and strong handle is the best size to buy. I maintain a bevel of approximately 45 degrees and remove the sharp corners the makers provide by grinding two long blades on the top of the gouge.

Although I love to use the bowl gouge for spindle turning, particularly for long flowing curves on goblets and vases, its main use is for bowls and facework. It is important to constantly rub the bevel to support and steady the cutting edge around external and internal curves. Cutting with the tip unsupported by the bevel makes it 'grabby' and prone to digging in.

To find the right position, lay the bevel on the wood (making sure the tool is firmly on the tool rest) so that you are in the 'no cut' position. With the bevel in contact with the rotating wood, slowly raise the handle until a shaving appears. Stay with it and guide it along or around the surface of the object you are making. You will soon appreciate the supported feeling that the bevel provides as the gouge tip cuts. REMEMBER, if you are changing the shape of the wood from a square corner to a curve, it is much easier if you cut away the corner to a wide chamfer first. To cut wood without the bevel rubbing is like driving a car without wheels!

All the tools that I have just written about are cutting tools which are usually used in an upward mode. The SKEW chisel is the exception as by raising the tool rest it is used mainly with the toolrest in the 'level with centre' position.

I would strongly recommend that you buy good quality tools. For the tools we have discussed so far — ROUGHING GOUGE, PARTING TOOL, SKEW CHISEL, SPINDLE GOUGE and BOWL GOUGE — I feel that it is worth the extra cost to purchase high speed steel. Tools of high speed steel will hold their edge up to five times longer and will not be affected like carbon steel by overheating from the electric grindstone.

The last of the basic tools to talk about are SCRAPERS, which are mainly used to remove any bumps and ridges left after using the Bowl Gouge. A scraper is used in a downward position with the tool rest set back from the work to give room to use it at this angle. When sharpened correctly, a sharp burr of metal stands up proud on the end of the tool which will produce plenty of shavings.

I have found that carbon steel scrapers, which are less expensive than high speed steel, work extremely well. The burr can be raised by pressing a hard metal bar across the end of the scraper which forces the cutting edge burr upwards (this is known as using a ticketer).

Scrapers can be made in different shapes. For faceplate work a square ended scraper, say 1" to 1 1/4" across with the corners relieved to allow the movement of the tool from the centre to the edge of flat surfaces and vice versa, is ideal. By grinding the corners back slightly, snagging is avoided when in use. For inside bowls and open vessels a 1" to 1 1/4" ROUND NOSED SCRAPER is ideal. The metal should be as sturdy as possible to avoid vibration when cantilevering inside a bowl on the tool rest.

Sharpening the Tools

The SKEW CHISEL and the PARTING TOOL only need re-grinding occasionally and honing with a slipstone is all that is required but keep them sharp at all times. A slipstone made from metal impregnated with diamond dust is an effective way of sharpening them.

I sharpen the end of the ROUGHING GOUGE to a shallow bevel of approximately 45 degree - REMEMBER, although useful for turning softwood etc. long bevels are more grabby for beginners to use. Be very careful to keep the blade straight across by rolling the tool over on the grinding wheel from one corner to the other. A common fault with new turners is only to sharpen the rounded part of the cutting edge which, if done for several sharpenings, forms two long points like cats ears on the gouge.

I sharpen the SPINDLE GOUGE to a finger nail shape with a bevel angle of somewhere between 45 degrees to 60 degrees. If you hold the gouge upwards and rotate it on the grindstone from left to right you will very quickly form a sharp point on the Spindle Gouge and lose the rounded profile. To avoid this rotate the tool, sharpening from centre to right, following the existing finger nail shape. You will find that in doing this when you start (with the handle straight and in line with the grindwheel) when you finish the handle will be approximately 45 degrees to the right of you. Now repeat this process from the centre to the left. ALWAYS use only light pressure — only a small touch on the stone is required. It is a good idea to practice this manoeuvre with the grinder switched off first.

The BOWL GOUGE is sharpened in much the same way but if you want the cut back profile I use on my bowl gouges, start from the middle and, following the edge of the tip profile, roll the gouge right over so the flute is facing the wheel, pushing it upwards. Then, to sharpen the cutback section, sharpen as before going toward the other side.

I always use SCRAPERS with the manufacturer's name uppermost so I know which way to use it; however, when sharpening these tools on the grindstone, I turn them upside down. Because the stone is rotating toward you and downwards, it naturally forms a good burr on the bottom edge of the tool which, of course, becomes the top when you use it.

Your grindstone should be kept at a sensible height so that you can use it without stooping. Mine is about 4' from the ground. It is a great help to have an anglepoise light on the stone. The following safety tips should be observed:

(1) NEVER use a grinder without eye protection e.g. visor, goggles or safety glasses. I find that those little clear plastic windows that are provided very soon get scratched and become impossible to see through.

(2) NEVER work on a grindstone that is clogged or out of true. Diamond Wheel Trimmers are much less expensive now and they clean the stone and trim it in just a couple of passes. REMEMBER a clean stone cuts cooler and sharpens efficiently. Take precautions by wearing a mask when trimming the stone as a large amount of dangerous dust is created when this is done.

(3) NEVER ever use your grindstone on soft or non ferrous metals such as copper or brass. If the stone is clogged with this type of material it can overheat with use and even shatter.

An alternative method for sharpening tools now being sold by a major British tool maker consists of wooden discs mounted on an arbor with aluminium oxide abrasives adhered to them. These can be held in a chuck on the lathe and you can clearly see what you are doing. The recommended speed is around 1400 r.p.m on a 5" disc.

Using the Lathe

Spindle Turning (or Turning Between Centres)

As a general rule I prefer to turn small diameter work (say up to 2" x 2") at a fairly fast speed. If you are reducing square stock to round, this makes the task quicker and avoids excess vibration being transferred through the tool to the joints in your hand.

Let us assume you have a piece of square timber mounted securely between centres. Select a speed of around 1200 to 1500 r.p.m. If we look at the pulleys contained within the headstock when selecting our turning speed, it is important to note that the smaller the size of the pulley, the faster the speed of the lathe will be. Put on your visor or safety goggles — ALWAYS PROTECT YOUR EYES.

Always avoid inhaling wood dust when sanding. Use a mask and an extraction unit. An airstream helmet is good but will not prevent a build up of fine dust in your workshop.

To mount the wood between centres when I am teaching, I use a ring centre or friction drive as opposed to a 2 or 4-prong drive. This method is safer because if you have a 'dig in' the wood will stop rotating and slip on the centres. A pronged drive keeps on going regardless and a heavy 'dig in' will result in chunks of wood flying off or the whole piece leaving the lathe. If you do not possess a friction drive, reduce the tension on the drive belt. This will also provide a safety mechanism.

Adjust your tool rest to around 1/2" below centre. Rotate the wood by hand before switching on to make sure it clears the tool rest. Then check all securing levers or nuts including the headstock swivel (applicable on rotating head lathes only) — the tool rest support to the lathe bed — the tailstock to the lathe bed and finally the securing lever to the quill of the tailstock.

Using a 3/4" or 1" Roughing Gouge, point the cutting edge upwards away from the rotating wood onto the tool rest. NOTE — NEVER place any turning tool onto the wood unless the tool is sitting firmly on the tool rest first. Now, gently lower the tip of the gouge until the bevel (flat area next to the cutting edge) is rubbing on the rotating wood without cutting. As lightly as possible (I call this the no-cut position), and still with the gouge on the rest, lift the back hand up and look for the finest of shavings. Use only light pressure toward the wood and obtain a light buzz from the cutting edge as you ease the tool along the tool rest and back.

Stand in nice and close to the lathe with your feet apart and use body movement to move the tool from left to right and vice versa. REMEMBER, outstretched arms are wobbly things. Keep the inside part of your arm against your side and move the tool along with body movement only. As soon as a gap of, say, no more than 1/2" appears between the tool rest and the wood, stop the lathe and move the tool rest in as close as you can while checking that the wood rotates freely without rubbing on the tool rest.

Switch on and, while looking at the horizon (top edge of the wood), make a nice smooth cylinder. Do not allow the tool to swing — this will give you a bad shape. Obtain a shaving, keep the tool at this angle, and move along the tool rest.

A ring centre, seen in place here on the lathe, is the best centre for beginners. It is most forgiving if you have a dig in.

The smaller the pulley on the headstock, the faster the work is going to go.

Mark the centre of the blank with a small hole made with an awl. On softer woods, tighten up the tail stock until the drive center grips. For a harder piece of wood, we might have to tap it with a hammer to begin to drive it into the wood.

Before you turn on the lathe, rotate the wood by hand to make sure that it is not hitting the tool rest. The top of the tool rest should be positioned approximately 3/4" below the centre. This height will vary according to the diameter of the timber, the height of the lathe, and the comfortable working postion the turner wishes to adopt.

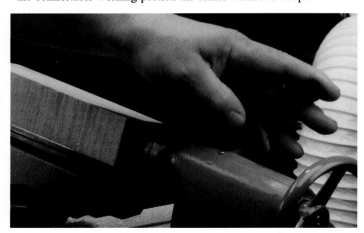

Double check all of the locking handles to the tail stock, and the tool rest, making sure they are tight. This precaution will help you avoid accidents. If your lathe is of the swivel head type, make sure the swivel nut is tightened as well. Otherwise, the head could turn while the wood is spinning.

The Roughing Gouge:

Let's look at the tools now. The first of the tools is the roughing gouge. For people first learning to turn, the roughing gouge is much easier to use if the bevel edge is kept short, approximately at 45 degrees. Longer bevels may be preferred as a turner become more experienced. But in the hands of someone new to wood turning, a long bevel is both grabby and more difficult to use.

The roughing gouge should be kept straight across at its cutting edge. I will explain this in detail later when we cover tool sharpening.

Begin with the tool in the "no cut" position.

Raise your arm, lifting the handle until the blade just touches the wood and begins to form shavings.

Slowly move along the length of the wood. Only light pressure is required with a sharp tool. As you move along the wood, roughing the corners off, all you should hear is a light buzz. That is the sign that you are doing the job correctly, making a nice spray of shavings as you go. Keep the tool firmly on the tool rest. Ensure that the bevel of the tool is always rubbing against the wood. This stablizes the tool for you and makes it safer to handle. Your tools will also not need to be sharpened as often. Someone new to wood turning tends to stand a long way out from the lathe, working with arms extended. This position tends to make the tool vibrate and wobble, making it hard to get a nice finish. Move in close. Keep your lower arm (the one holding the lower part of the handle) resting against your body, using your body to move the tool back and forth.

If you travel too fast, rifling will occur. Spiral grooves are created all along the wood.

Remember, the slower you go, the nicer the finish. Half of the rifling has been removed in this picture.

The roughing gouge is mainly used to reduce square stock to round and for truing up unbalanced timber. However, the roughing gouge is also a useful tool for shaping shallow curves and hollows. Always work down the hill (from the largest to the smallest diameter). By doing this, you are compressing the fibers of the wood together and cutting the wood as it likes to be cut; cutting uphill will separate the wood fibers and give you an inferior finish.

The Parting Tool:

A good parting tool to start turning with is a 1/8" parting tool. Later on, you may feel like investing in a diamond profile 3/16" parting tool (seen on the left) which moves more easily through the wood, without a tendency to be gripped. The diamond profile is, of course, also a much stronger tool for deeper cuts.

While parting the wood, never allow the tool to fall below the centerline position because it can be pulled in by the rotating wood and get caught between the wood and the tool rest.

The approach to the wood, as before, is from a high position with the bevel rubbing. Lift the handle upwards and lower the cutting edge gently down onto the surface of the wood. Continue cutting into it, then go back to the starting position again and take a second cut alongside the first to widen the groove. This will prevent your tool being grabbed in a narrow parting cut. The first use of this tool is to remove the scrap wood from either end of the piece. There are two reasons for doing this. One is to remove the marks left by the drive and live centers and the other is to ensure that the wood is cut away on the end of the piece of timber. This area is often full of small hair cracks where it has dried.

The second use of the parting tool is with it sitting firmly on the tool rest, the bevel rubbing, pushing upwards only. Again, widen the groove as before to keep the tool from being gripped.

Cut down the diameter of the waste wood so that it is a little larger than the lathe centers. This will keep the waste wood out of our way, giving us better access to the ends of the wood.

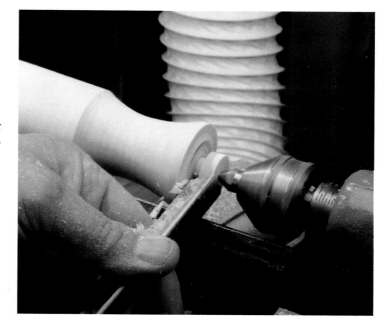

The parting tool is also very useful when forming beads. The wider the parting tool, the easier it is to use for this function. Make two shallow grooves, one on either side of the proposed bead. Place the parting tool, with the bevel rubbing, in the centre of the bead-to-be and, with a rolling action, roll over to the right two or three times until you have rounded over the square corner on the right.

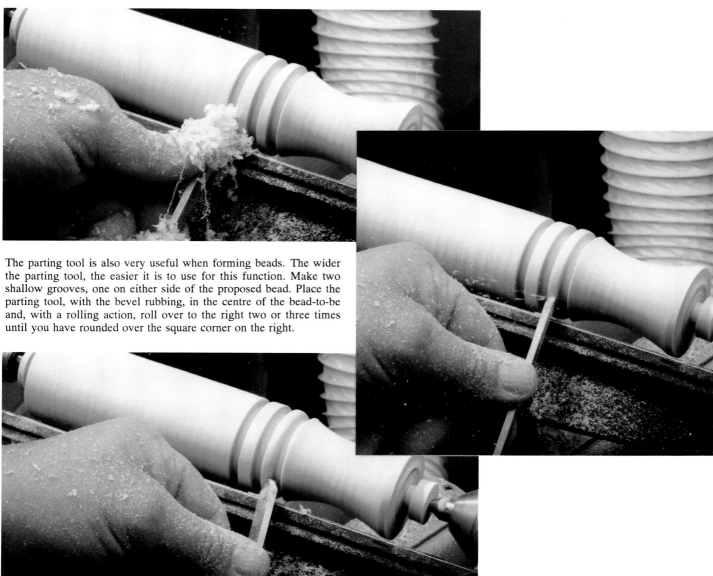

Then move to the left to round the other side. Remember, always look at the horizon to obtain the best view of the shapes you are making.

The parting tool has one other useful function. Placed on its side, flat on the tool rest in a downward scraping mode, it is excellent for making fine decorative lines and grooves.

The spindle gouge is generally used for shaping wood and forming coves and beads. It can also be used to clean up end grain. The best spindle gouge for beginners is the 3/8". To make a cove, start with the bevel rubbing, supporting the cutting edge, and swing the handle in a perfect circular motion. If the handle travels in a circle, your cove will be round. Smooth flowing actions are key to making nice shapes.

With the parting tool, we can further enhance the appearance of the cove by cutting two small shoulders, one on either side. This gives the cove a classical look often found in beautiful period furniture.

The Skew Chisel:

Raise the tool rest to the lathe centre height or just above centre to use the skew chisel.

I would suggest you buy a 1" oval skew chisel. You will find this tool much nicer to handle and much smoother to run along the tool rest than the old style square edged skew chisel. The square corners tend to catch in all the marks in the tool rest. The oval chisel glides across them.

Use the short corner of the skew for planing the wood. We are only going to use the area 1/8" from the short corner. Do not cut with the higher part of the blade.

First put your thumb slightly to the right of the starting position on the tool rest. Lay the bevel of the tool on the wood, raising a shaving just above the short corner.

Slide the tool along the tool rest in a planing action. If the tool judders and doesn't run smoothly, either raise or lower your back hand slightly or change the angle of your cut very slightly. When you feel it is right, continue with the planing action.

The skew chisel is used for rounding over ends, for forming balls and for beads. To round the end you must rub the bevel along the edge of the wood.

Using the skew chisel to make beads.

Using the skew chisel to make a ball. Work first to the right and then to the left, bringing the ball into shape on both sides equally.

The Round Nosed Scraper:

Buy a 1" or 1 1/4" round nosed scraper manufactured from good, sturdy metal. The scraper doesn't have to be made of high speed steel. The round nosed scraper, used in the downward angle, is ideal for cleaning up, removing tool marks, smoothing down troublesome end grain, and is invaluable when face plate or bowl turning.

The Bowl Gouge:

A 3/8" bowl gouge is a good size to start with in your tool kit. You can see how large it is.

Sharpening the tools using an electric grinding wheel:

Sharpening the roughing gouge. Make sure the top is straight across.

It is essential that your grindstone is fixed at a sensible height where you can view what you are doing without stooping. Standard work bench height is far too low for most people. The grindstone should also be well lit. Light is an essential aid when examining a tool for sharpness: a blunt section of the blade will reflect light and a sharp section will not. I prefer not to use the manufacturer's see-through shields. I find they soon become scuffed and marked and are very difficult to see through. Always wear safety goggles or glasses while working on the grindstone. This is very important. Always ensure that your grinding wheel is running true and that it is clean. Both of these functions can be achieved with the use of a diamond (or other form of) trimmer.

Sharpening the spindle gouge. Refer to the notes in the general material for further sharpening details.

Turning for the Garden

The three objects to be created during these projects. The garden dibber
is shown in front, the planter is on the right, and the bird box is shown
on the left.

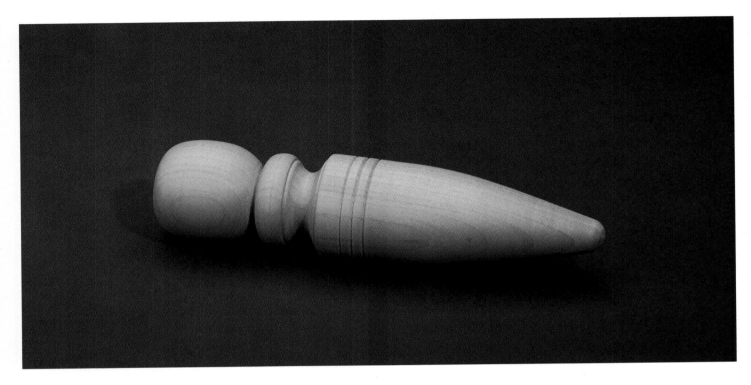

The Garden Dibber

The Garden Dibber: producing this dibber is a spindle turning project with the wood supported between the two lathe centers. This is a piece of Maple but any good quality hardwood that is known to weather well would be suitable. The Maple block measures 9" long x 2" square. First find the centres. Mark them in pencil at both ends.

Mark the centre with an awl.

20

I'm going to use a ring centre instead of a 4 or 2 prong drive center. In England where I do a lot of teaching of wood turning to beginners the ring drive is invaluable as a safety aid and can be set to slip by adjusting the tail stock to the resistance required. The ring centre is also used by professional turners when they are producing repetitive turnings of the same size. With the ring centre they can place pieces on the lathe and remove them without switching the motor off.

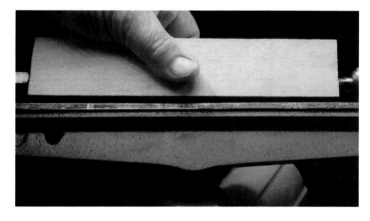

Begin with your roughing gouge in the "no cut" position.

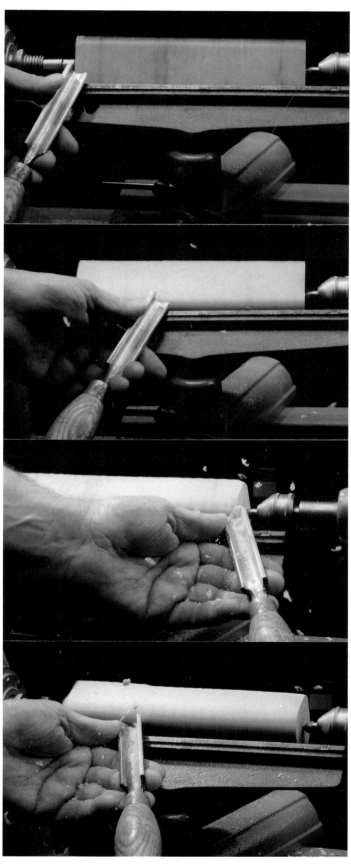

Mount the wood with the tool rest about 3/4" below center. Turn the wood by hand to ensure that it clears the tool rest.

Bring the blade up until you get the first sign of a shaving. Slide the gouge along the tool rest, changing the angle when you get to the other end to come back from right to left.

Continue this process until the wood is reduced to a true cylinder. When a wide gap is formed between the tool rest and the reduced wood, it is essential that the lathe is stopped and the tool rest is move in as close as possible to the work.

The wood has been reduced to a true cylinder. Mark off the waste wood ends with a pencil while the lathe is rotating.

We are now going to separate the waste wood with a deep parting cut. We do this because we don't want to use the pieces of wood on the ends which have the centre marks in them. It is also good practice to have waste wood on the end as pieces of wood that sit on the shelf for a long time tend to form small drying cracks in the ends.

Every time you cut, widen the gap so the parting tool does not bind.

Reduce the parting spigot down to 3/8" in diameter.

Reduce the waste wood beyond the parting cut until it is a little bigger than the center. Repeat this at the other end.

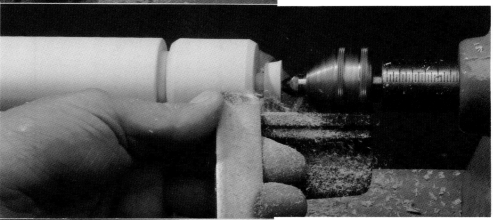

Now mark out a groove in pencil which separates an area approximately the diameter of the thickness of the wood from the rest of the piece. We are going to make a shallow groove along the pencil line with the parting tool. Then we will form a ball which will be the top of our garden dibber, the part that is in the palm of your hand when the dibber is in use.

Raise the tool rest and use the skew chisel to round the ball. Whatever you do to the right hand side, do to the left when making a ball. First round the sharp edges with the skew chisel, using a smooth rocking motion.

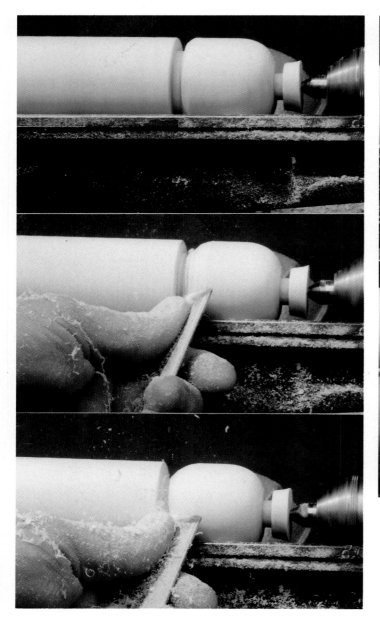

When you make a ball (or any shape equal on both sides), work a bit on the right and a bit on the left so that you bring on the shape gradually and equally. When you are nearing completion, stand back and look at the shape to make sure it is correct. A final small adjustment is usually necessary to make a shape you are pleased with. Continue rounding in. Finally round the flattened centre with very small movements.

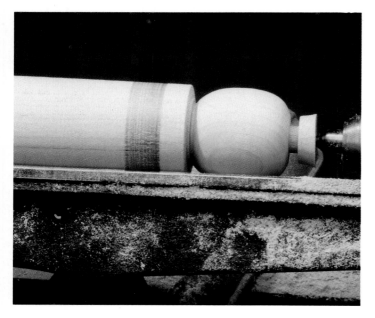

Now we are going to make a cove or hollow at this mark.

With the parting tool, make a shallow groove as shown in the picture. This is a great benefit to inexperienced turners who may experience some problems with the spindle gouge slipping out either side of the cove. These ledges on either side give you something for the tool to rest against. We are working with the tool rest 3/4" below center, having dropped it from above centre where we were using the skew.

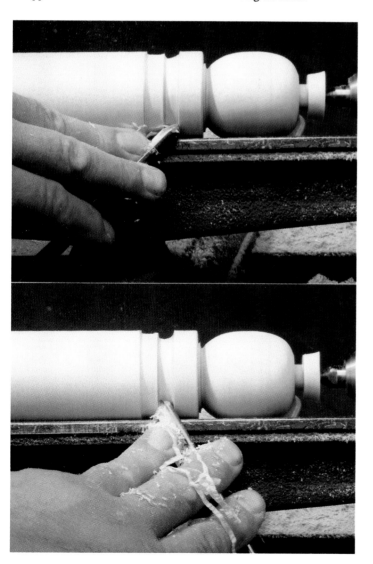

Form the cove by coming down the right side ...

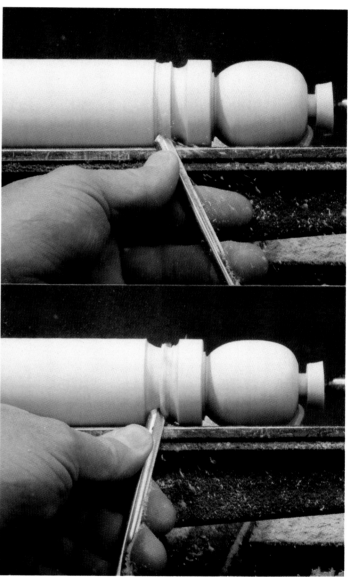

... and then the left.

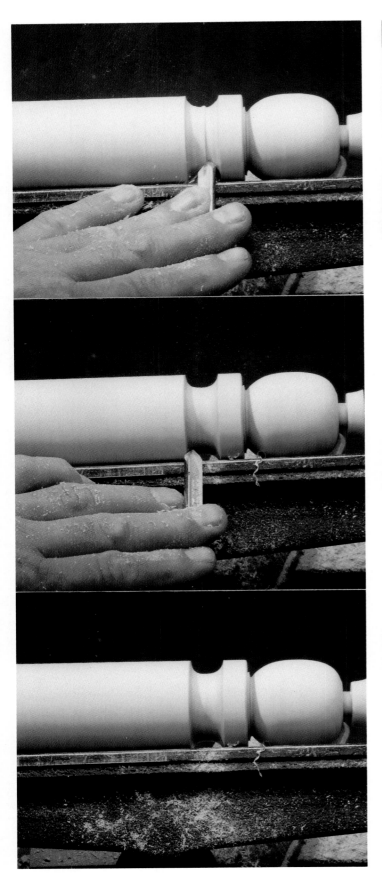

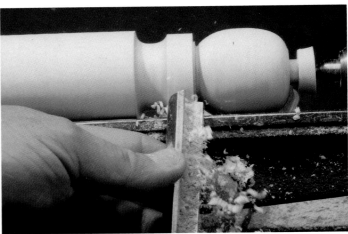

Reduce the size of the bead slightly using a roughing gouge.

Remember to cut down hill to obtain the best finish. Remember if your handle travels in smooth circles then your cove will have smooth contours.

Round the sharp edges around the cove and bead with the parting tool.

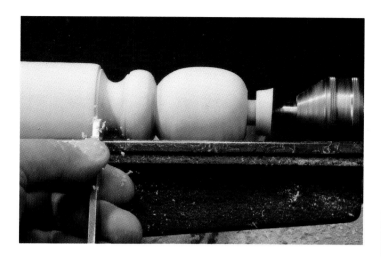

Put in small shoulders on either side of the cove.

We are now going to cut a taper. The first thing we do is to reduce the wood at the thinnest end of the dibber.

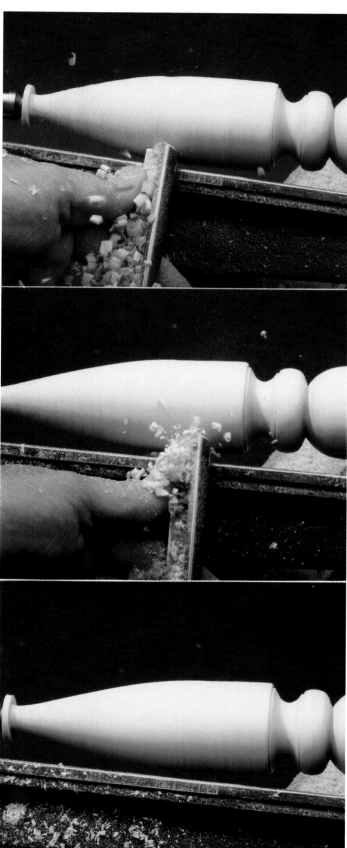

Gradually tapering it down, moving toward the widest end using the 3/4" roughing gouge.

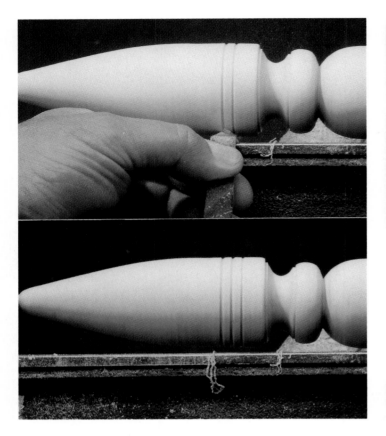

Using the parting tool on its side as a scraper in a downward mode scoring some decorative lines.

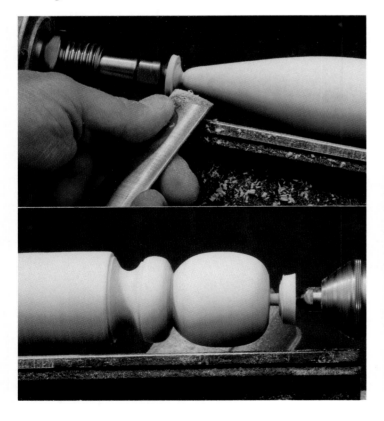

Finally we turn over the pointed end of the dibber to a rounded shape with a skew chisel and we part in adjacent to the ball a the other end to a thickness of 3/16" approximately.

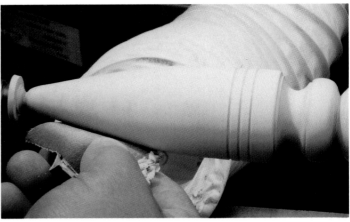

Remove the tool rest completely when sanding. Otherwise your fingers can be pulled in against the rest during sanding operations. Sand the dibber with cloth backed abrasive strips, gradually working from the coarsest to the finest grades, taking care not to round down the sharp edges of your shoulders. Always use a dust extractor to keep your lungs and your shop clean. Place some shavings within the abrasive strip to keep from burning your fingers. Move the abrasive from left to right continually while sanding to avoid scratching the dibber.

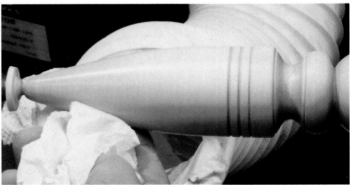

As this dibber is for outdoor use, we will only put on several coats of oil and no wax. Apply Danish Oil (or the sealer of your choice) to the dibber with a brush and buff with a paper towel.

Remove the dibber from the lathe and cut off the waste wood spigots. Sand the ends and coat them with oil to finish the dibber.

The finished dibber.

The Garden Planter

The Garden Planter

Our second project uses a piece of unseasoned American Black Walnut in the round. We are making a planter for the garden. Attach a face plate to the wood. Slow down the speed of your lathe before proceeding with this project.

Attach the unseasoned Walnut to the lathe. It is most important to bring up the tail stock and insert the live centre firmly into the log. We must SLOW THE LATHE RIGHT DOWN. Start off around 600 to 800 R.P.M. which can be increased to 1000 to 1200 R.P.M. when the blank has been trued up. As we are going to be cutting away the bark from the log, wear a protective visor. Insert the tool rest, turn the wood by hand to make sure the wood clears the rest and begin to reduce the bark with a heavy bowl gouge.

Work in from the right end, gradually bringing the tool rest closer in. On many lathes, the rest will not fit beneath the log until it has been trued up, as you can see here. As the log begins to true up, you may also gradually increase the speed of the lathe. Speed the lathe up too much, too fast though and the lathe will chase you around the room. If you intend to do a lot of heavy work using unbalanced timber, bolt the lathe to the floor permanently.

Now the wood is trued up far enough to get the tool rest in under it. It is also necessary, from time to time, to tighten up the tail stock as this is a soft piece of wood.

Use the heavy roughing gouge to further improve the shape of the log.

We have cut our way through the bark and through a large proportion of the pithy sap wood surrounding the timber.

We are truing this shape up to receive the expanding jaws of the chuck. We will form a recess to receive the chuck when we reverse the piece to hollow it out.

True up the top edge by the face plate to remove ragged edges and true up the shape of the bowl, parting a groove at the edge of the waste wood using the bowl gouge. A final cut over the surface with the roughing gouge will smooth the bowl.

Using the parting tool, create a decorative bead at the top. First cut a groove and then round both sides of the bead. The lower edge is rounded into the groove and the upper edge is rounded at the top of the bead and bowl.

Using the roughing gouge to reduce the size of the bowl below the bead.

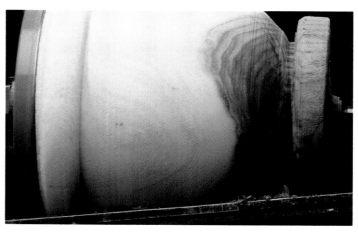

The piece is now ready to receive the chuck recess. We have done as much preshaping as we can.

True up the end of the planter with the roughing gouge. Be careful with the centre spigot, it must be removed in small stages.

The end is trued up, ready to prepare to fit the chuck.

Reduce away the centre to the 1/4" depth with the roughing tool.

Mark out the diameter of the chuck jaws with the dividers. Do not allow the right hand tip of the divider to touch the wood or that end will be flipped over to the left by the direction of the lathe's spin.

Put in an undercut to fit the shape of the chuck jaws.

Open up a recess 1/4" deep with the parting gouge.

Sand the end to harden up the surface.

in your library. We would like to keep you informed about other publications from Schiffer Publishing Ltd.

TITLE OF BOOK: _____   ☐ hardcover
                                           ☐ paperback

☐ Bought at: _____
☐ Received as gift _____

COMMENTS: _____

_____

_____

Name *(please print clearly)* _____

Address _____

City _____ State _____ Zip _____

☐ *Please send me a free Schiffer Arts, Antiques & Collectibles catalog.*

☐ *Please send me a free Schiffer Woodcarving, Woodworking & Crafts catalog*

☐ *Please send me a free Schiffer Military/Aviation History catalog*

☐ *Please send me a free Whitford Press Mind, Body & Spirit and Donning Pictorials &*

   Cookbooks catalog.

SCHIFFER BOOKS ARE CURRENTLY AVAILABLE FROM YOUR BOOKSELLER

SCHIFFER PUBLISHING LTD
77 LOWER VALLEY RD
ATGLEN PA 19310-9717

Apply a generous coat of oil to the bottom. This will prevent cracking.

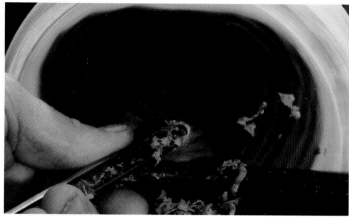

Use a bowl gouge to begin recessing the bowl from the centre outward. Also reduce away the waste wood at this end of the planter. Make sure the bevel always rubs against the wood as you hollow out the center.

Insert the chuck onto the end of the lathe and fit the chuck jaws into the planter's newly formed recess. We are now ready to hollow out the planter.

Remove the face plate.

Because we are cutting end grain, all we get are short bits of fiber rather than long shavings.

If you prefer to cut with long shavings, I will show you an alternative method. What we will do is drill a hole deep into the vessel using the tail stock and drill chuck. We will then use a ring tool to cut sideways from the hole to widen the hole and produce those shavings we all like.

When you have gone as far as the tail stock will allow, wind back the quill of the tail stock entirely and move the tail stock forward.

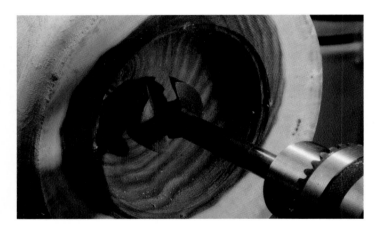

We are now going to drill a hole using a 1 1/2" inch sawtooth cutter in a drill chuck in the tail stock. When using these types of cutters, the secrets of drilling well are slow speed and high pressure. Drilling too fast will blue the tips and effect the temper in the steel.

The tail stock has been moved forward and is ready to drill again.

Drilling the centre of the planter with the sawtooth cutter.

Move the tail stock forward with the quill retracted to fully bottom out on the hole drilled already.

We are going to be using the 1/2" ring tool to cut sideways on the hole we have just made. This picture shows you how the ring tool has the same cutting action as the roughing gouge facing sideways, which of course is an impossible situation.

The 1/2" ring tool begins to cut out the hole.

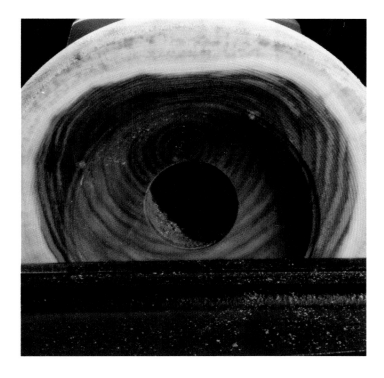

The completed drill hole.

Progress. Notice the nice long shavings.

Nearing completion.

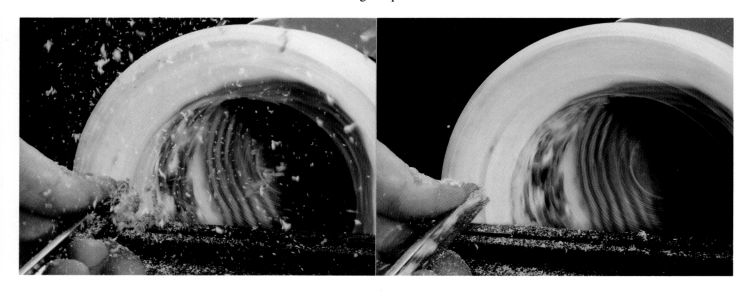

Use the 3/8" bowl gouge to round the outer edge. The ring tool can get grabby along this outer edge. Gradually round down into the bowl from the edge.

The inside of the planter bowl is nearly complete.

Go back in with the ring tool to clean up the rough surfaces.

Blending in the bowl and rim with the scraper held at 45 degrees (sheer scraping).

Sand down the bowl.

The sanded bowl.

Add a nice heavy coat of oil or sealer.

True up the outside with the bowl gouge.

Roll over the edge of the bowl gouge as you approach the rim, like this.

Sand down the outside of the planter.

Apply a coat of Danish Oil or sealer to the planter.

The finished planter.

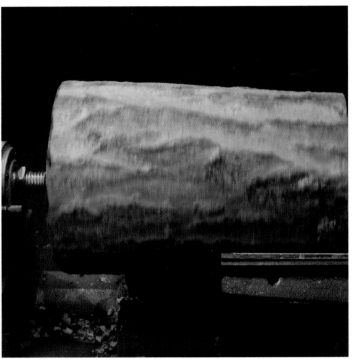

The log is mounted on the lathe. Set it at a slow speed for obvious safety reasons.

Begin to true up the log. As you go (and the log diminishes in size), you will be able to move the tool rest under the log.

For our third project, we will make a bird box (bird house) out of a Red Oak log. True up the ends of the log on the bandsaw, mark out the centers, and drive in a good, heavy four prong drive.

Time to true up the ends. Mark them in pencil and part them slightly with the parting tool to give you an edge to work to.

Watch the top horizon as you work to get an idea of the actual shape.

Begin truing up the ends with the bowl gouge. You need a nice flat surface to attach the face plate to.

Make sure the end is flat. Round the corner of the log so as not to hurt your hands ...

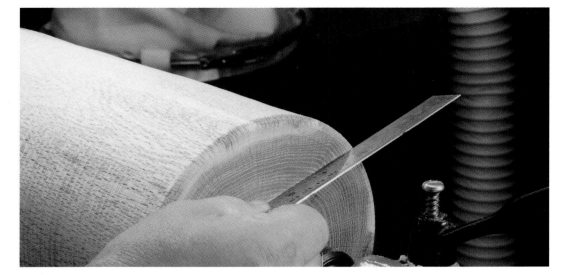

... and attach the face plate with strong screws.

Mount the face plate on the lathe and true up the wood again with the roughing gouge.

True up the end of the log with a bowl gouge.

A 2 1/2" spigot to hold the lid in the chuck jaws made with a combination of a parting tool and a 3/8" bowl gouge.

Mark the separation between the lid and the bird box (or nest box) itself.

Now cut deeply into the wood, creating a separation between the lid and the box.

Using the parting tool, separate the lid from the box.

Round the lid with the 3/8" bowl gouge.

Like this.

I have formed the bird's access hole using a drill press. I have also made a small hole to one side below it for a perch to enable the proposed occupant to have a look 'round before hopping in.

Using the 1 1/2" sawtooth bit in the drill chuck in the tail stock, drill a hole down to the level of the chuck itself.

Clean up the end before proceeding.

Widening the hole enough to accept the nose of the chuck holding the sawtooth bit. This allows the drill to penetrate a bit deeper.

We are drilling down the centre so that we may once again use the ring tool. You will need to adjust the tail stock as before when you reach its maximum extension.

The hole is drilled.

Taper the box with the roughing gouge. The lid must be larger than the box to keep water off the box.

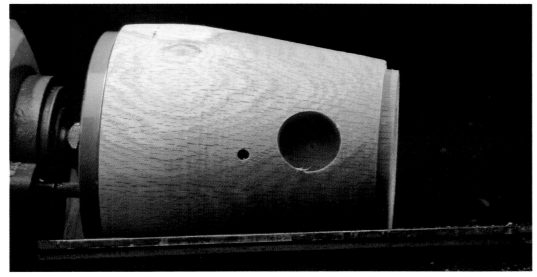

The top is tapered and the end is reduced with the parting tool to accept the lid tightly.

Widen the opening in the top with the 3/8" bowl gouge to make access easier for the 1/2" ring gouge.

Continue rounding out the centre of the box with the ring gouge.

Using a scraper tip to smooth down the sides and base inside the box.

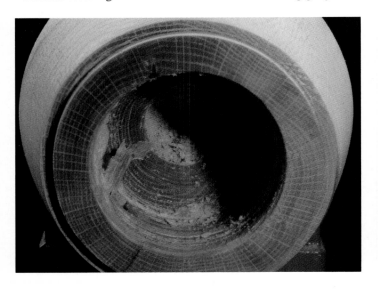

Making progress.

The inside is rounded.

Using the ring gouge.

Use the parting tool to cut away some of the waste wood below the bottom of the box. Watch out for the face plate mounting screws.

Sand the bird box with the abrasive strips. Remember to line them with shavings so as not to burn your fingers. You may sand the inside of the box as well by wrapping a abrasive strip around a paint stirring stick or similar object.

Round the bottom of the bird box with the bowl gouge.

Add a little oil to the wood, remove the base from the face plate, attach the open end of the bird box to the chuck jaws, and support the bottom with the tail stock. Reduce the excess wood and shape the base of the box using a bowl gouge.

Remove the remaining waste wood with a parting gouge and sand the bottom of the bird box. Keep the abrasive strip moving so as not to score the wood.

Add oil and remove the bird box from the chuck jaws.

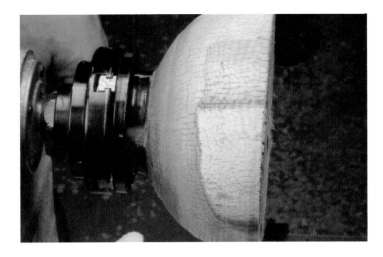

Moving on to the lid. Mount the lid on the lathe, using the spigot we prepared.

Transfer this measurement to the underside of the lid.

Clean off the underside of the lid with a gouge.

Cut in straight with the parting tool along the marked line. Then round the interior with the bowl gouge to fit over the lip on the box and provide a little extra room for tall birds.

Measure the diameter of lip of the bird box opening. Keep this measurement loose, giving you a little wiggle room.

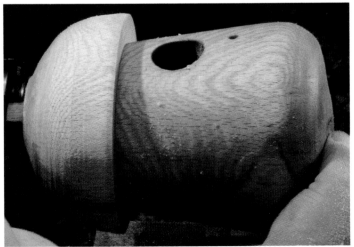

The lid fits.

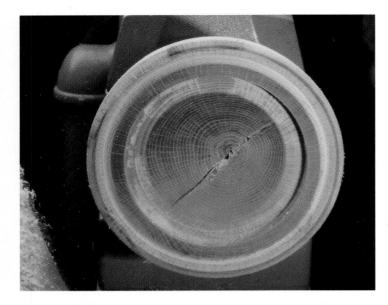

Use the parting tool on its side as a scraper to add a drip groove to divert rain from running along underneath the lid of the bird box (the outermost ring).

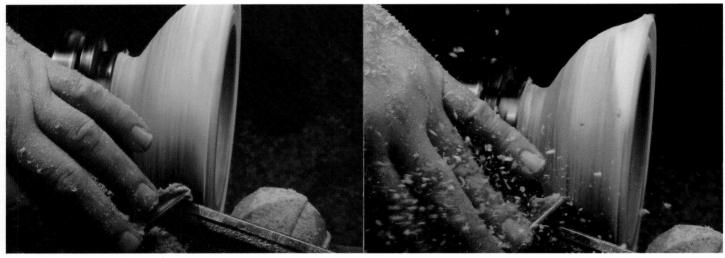

Refine the shape of the lid with the bowl gouge. The shape is similar to a thatched roof in England.

Reverse the lid, using a 4 prong drive and the tail stock to hold the lid in place. Use the parting tool to apply the small ridge near to top. A spike or a ball on the tip would also look good.

Bring the top to a small point and cut it loose from the spigot with the bowl gouge.

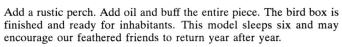

Add a rustic perch. Add oil and buff the entire piece. The bird box is finished and ready for inhabitants. This model sleeps six and may encourage our feathered friends to return year after year.

It is also fun to make a simple box left in its natural state with the bark on. Remember to keep the hole just below the lid.

Gallery

The completed projects.

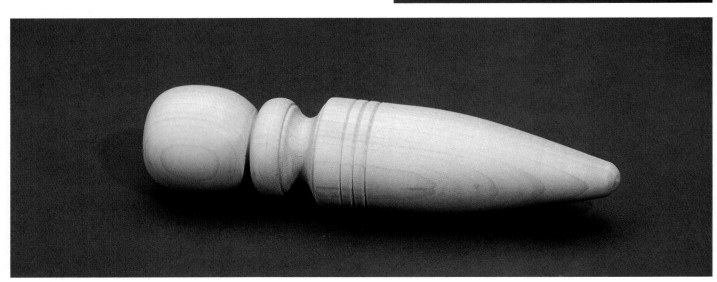

The Garden Dibber

The Garden Planter

The Bird Nesting Box

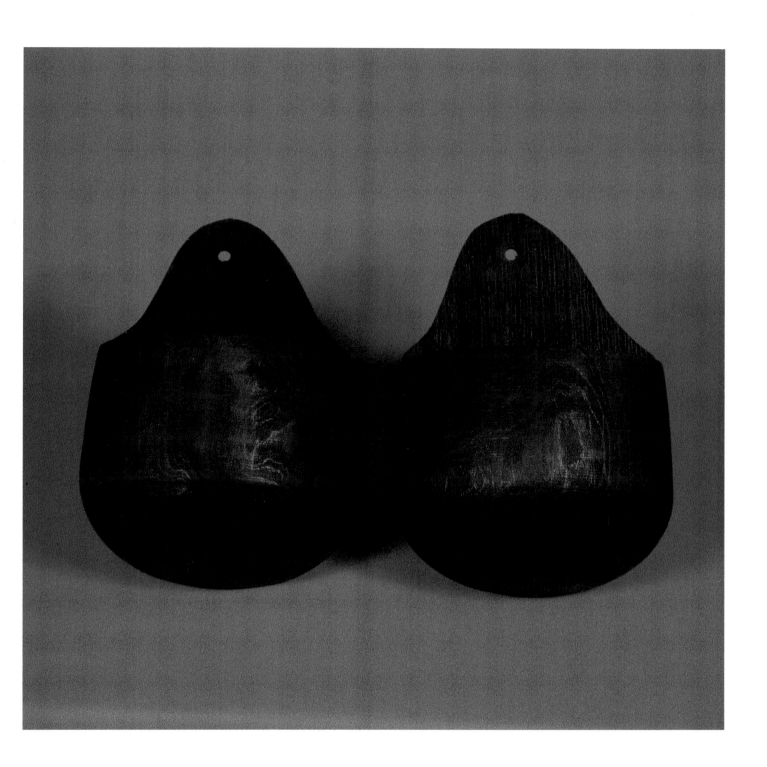